S0-BZU-306

Meet the

SAN DIEGO CHARGERS

BY

ZACK BURGESS

NORWOODHOUSE PRESS

CHICAGO, ILLINOIS

NORWOOD HOUSE PRESS

P.O. Box 316598 • Chicago, Illinois 60631
For more information about Norwood House Press please visit our website at
www.norwoodhousepress.com or call 866-565-2900.

Photo Credits:

All photos courtesy of Associated Press, except for the following: Topps, Inc. (6, 10 both, 22),
Black Book Archives (7, 15, 23), Fleer Corp. (11 top & bottom), McDonald's Corp. (11 middle),
NFL/Chargers (18).

Cover Photo: Kevin Terrell/Associated Press

The football memorabilia photographed for this book is part of the authors' collection. The collectibles used
for artistic background purposes in this series were manufactured by many different card companies—
including Bowman, Donruss, Fleer, Leaf, O-Pee-Chee, Pacific, Panini America, Philadelphia Chewing Gum,
Pinnacle, Pro Line, Pro Set, Score, Topps, and Upper Deck—as well as several food brands, including
Crane's, Hostess, Kellogg's, McDonald's and Post.

Designer: Ron Jaffe
Series Editors: Mike Kennedy and Mark Stewart
Project Management: Black Book Partners, LLC.
Editorial Production: Lisa Walsh

LIBRARY OF CONGRESS CATALOGING-IN-PUBLICATION DATA

Names: Burgess, Zack.
Title: Meet the San Diego Chargers / by Zack Burgess.
Description: Chicago, Illinois : Norwood House Press, 2016. | Series: Big
    picture sports | Includes bibliographical references and index.
Identifiers: LCCN 2015023900| ISBN 9781599537290 (library edition : alk.
    paper) | ISBN 9781603578325 (ebook)
Subjects: LCSH: San Diego Chargers (Football team)--History--Juvenile
    literature.
Classification: LCC GV956.S29 B87 2016 | DDC 796.332/6409794985--dc23
LC record available at http://lccn.loc.gov/2015023900

© 2017 by Norwood House Press. All rights reserved.
No part of this book may be reproduced without written permission from the publisher.
The San Diego Chargers is a registered trademark of San Diego Chargers Football Co.
This publication is not affiliated with the San Diego Chargers Football Co.,
The National Football League, or The National Football League Players Association.

288N—072016
Manufactured in the United States of America in North Mankato, Minnesota

CONTENTS

Words in **bold type** are defined on page 24.

The Chargers celebrate a "bolt from the blue."

4

CALL ME A CHARGER

Who says lightning never strikes twice? Just ask the San Diego Chargers. The bolts on their helmets and uniforms are proof of that. The Chargers love to light up the scoreboard. They can strike at any time from any place on the field.

TIME MACHINE

The Chargers play in California. After one year in Los Angeles in 1960, they moved to San Diego. The team won the championship of the **American Football League (AFL)** in 1963. The Chargers have had many star quarterbacks and receivers, including Dan Fouts and **Kellen Winslow**.

TE

KELLEN WINSLOW

Dan Fouts was the greatest passer in team history.

The Chargers' stadium is packed for a home game.

BEST SEAT IN THE HOUSE

The Chargers moved into a new stadium in 1967. Banners that honor the team's greatest players hang around the top of it. Many of these stars still come to games. The fans cheer when they are shown on the scoreboard.

SHOE BOX

The trading cards on these pages show some of the best Chargers ever.

LANCE ALWORTH

RECEIVER · 1962–1970

Lance was a track star in college. His speed and grace made him an AFL all-star seven years in a row.

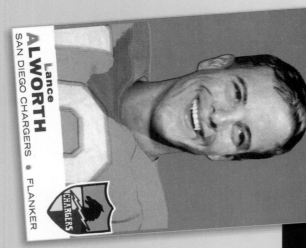

Lance **ALWORTH**
SAN DIEGO CHARGERS · FLANKER

DAN FOUTS

QUARTERBACK · 1973–1987

Dan had a strong arm and a quick mind. He passed for more than 4,000 yards each year from 1979 to 1981.

CHARGERS
DAN FOUTS

LESLIE O'NEAL

DEFENSIVE END · 1986–1995

Leslie had great speed and strength. He had more than 100 **quarterback sacks** for the Chargers.

JUNIOR SEAU

LINEBACKER · 1990–2002

Junior loved chess as a boy. This helped him figure out plays before they even started!

PHILIP RIVERS

QUARTERBACK · FIRST YEAR WITH TEAM: 2004

Philip always seemed to know what the defense was going to do. He set the team record for touchdown passes.

THE BIG PICTURE

Look at the two photos on page 13. Both appear to be the same. But they are not. There are three differences. Can you spot them?

Answers on page 23.

TRUE OR FALSE?

LaDainian Tomlinson was a star running back. Two of these facts about him are **TRUE**. One is **FALSE**. Do you know which is which?

1 LaDainian scored his 100th NFL touchdown faster than any player in history.

2 LaDainian's nickname was The "Great 'Dain."

3 In a 2005 game, LaDainian passed for a touchdown and also scored on a run and a catch.

Answer on page 23.

LaDainian Tomlinson charges through an opening in the defense.

The Chargers love spending time with their fans.

GO CHARGERS, GO!

Chargers fans have lots of fun at home games. The team's fight song is "San Diego Super Chargers." Fans first started singing it in 1979. Many players on the team grew up in California. They remember the song from when they were kids.

ON THE MAP

Here is a look at where five Chargers were born, along with a fun fact about each.

 CHARLIE JOINER · MANY, LOUISIANA
Charlie was voted into the **Hall of Fame** in 1996.

 KELLEN WINSLOW · ST. LOUIS, MISSOURI
Kellen led the NFL in catches twice.

 ANTONIO GATES · DETROIT, MICHIGAN
Antonio was a college basketball star before joining the Chargers.

 SHAWNE MERRIMAN · WASHINGTON, D.C.
Shawne was an **All-Pro** in 2006.

JEREMIAH ATTAOCHU · IBADAN, NIGERIA
In his second season, Jeremiah became one of the team's best defenders.

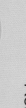

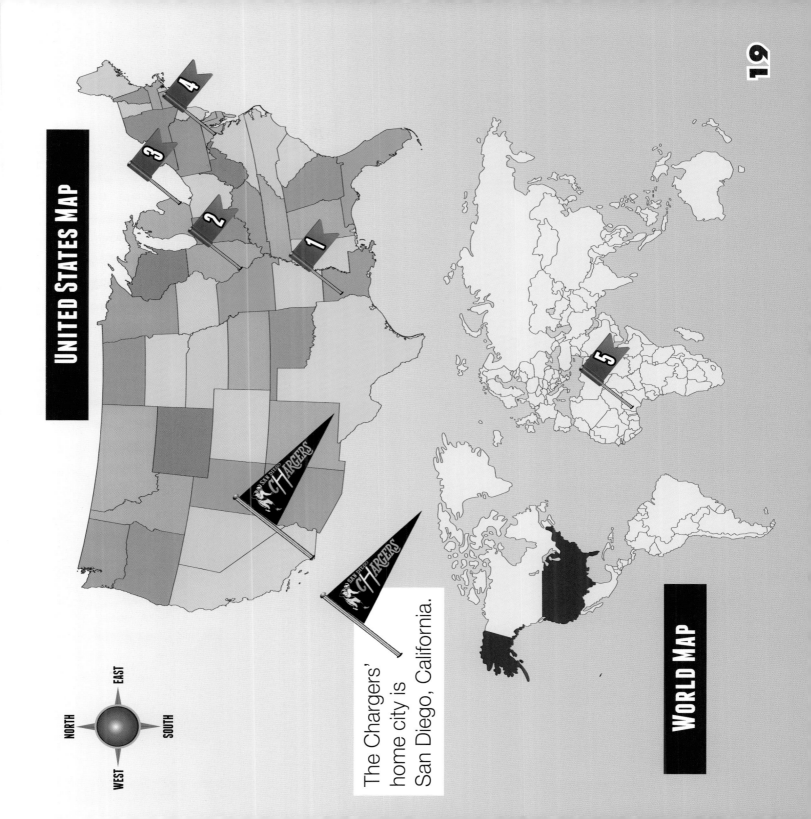

UNITED STATES MAP

NORTH
EAST
SOUTH
WEST

The Chargers' home city is San Diego, California.

WORLD MAP

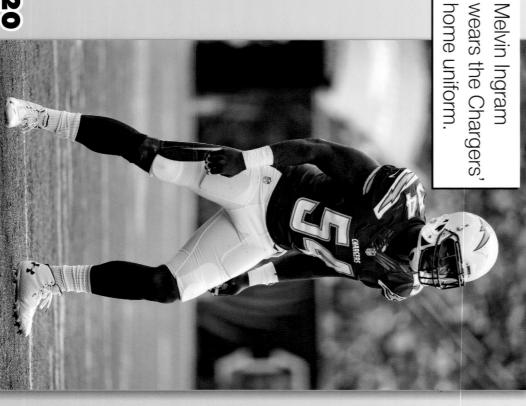

Melvin Ingram wears the Chargers' home uniform.

HOME AND AWAY

Football teams wear different uniforms for home and away games. The main colors of the Chargers are dark blue and white. Sometimes, they wear special light blue uniforms.

Manti Te'o wears the Chargers' away uniform.

The Chargers' helmet is easy to spot. It has a yellow lightning bolt on each side. The team also features lightning bolts on its uniforms.

WE WON!

The Chargers won the AFL championship in 1963. Coach Sid Gillman loved the passing game. But he also relied on running backs Paul Lowe and

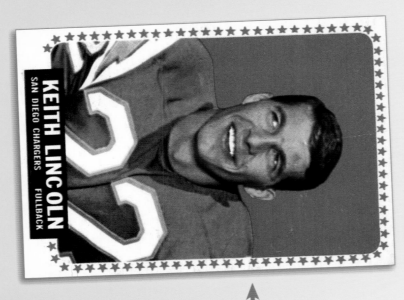

Keith Lincoln. The Chargers joined the National Football League in 1970. They played in their first Super Bowl in 1995.

KEITH LINCOLN
SAN DIEGO CHARGERS
FULLBACK

RECORD BOOK

These Chargers set team records.

COMPLETED PASSES

	RECORD
Season: Philip Rivers (2015)	437
Career: Philip Rivers	3,462

RECEIVING YARDS

	RECORD
Season: Lance Alworth (1965)	1,602
Career: **Antonio Gates**	10,644

POINTS

	RECORD
Season: LaDainian Tomlinson (2006)	186
Career: John Carney	1,076

ANSWERS FOR THE BIG PICTURE

#77 changed to #75, the lightning bolt on #17's pants changed to blue, and the socks of the player on the far right changed to light blue.

ANSWER FOR TRUE AND FALSE

#2 is false. LaDainian was not nicknamed the "Great 'Dain."

FOOTBALL WORDS

All-Pro
An honor given to the best NFL player at each position.

American Football League (AFL)
A rival league of the NFL that played from 1960 to 1969.

Hall of Fame
The museum in Canton, Ohio, where football's greatest players are honored.

Quarterback Sacks
Tackles of the quarterback that lose yardage.

INDEX

ABOUT THE AUTHOR

Zack Burgess has been writing about sports for more than 20 years. He has lived all over the country and interviewed lots of All-Pro football players, including Brett Favre, Eddie George, Jerome Bettis, Shannon Sharpe, and Rich Gannon. Zack was the first African American beat writer to cover Major League Baseball when he worked for the *Kansas City Star*.

ABOUT THE CHARGERS

Learn more at these websites:

www.chargers.com • www.profootballhof.com
www.teamspiritextras.com/Overtime/html/chargers.html